ARRIVA TRAINS WALES

Nicholas Wilcock

AMBERLEY

Front cover: On 25 July 2017, No. 150255 heads east along the Vale of Glamorgan line at Castle Upon Alun, between Bridgend and Llantwit Major while working 2A36, the 13:42 Bridgend to Aberdare service. This section of the Vale of Glamorgan line reopened to passengers in 2005 and is served by an hourly service.

Rear cover, top to bottom: Cardiff Queen St is very much the hub for Arriva's services in the Valleys and over recent years has been expanded to improve capacity. On 3 April 2017, Nos 143605 and 143622 depart with 2F31, the 10:47 Treherbert to Cardiff Central service.

Nos 142075 and 143623 stand at Penarth prior to working 2D54, the 15:32 service to Bargoed, on 14 September 2016.

No. 150267 stands at a rather colourful Pontyclun while working 2L54, the 13:15 Maesteg to Cardiff Central, on a sunny 15 August 2017.

No. 150267 heads west near Aberthaw Power Station on 20 January 2017 with a service bound for Bridgend via Barry along the Vale of Glamorgan line.

At the end of a day's services, No. 150252 stands at a deserted Cardiff Central having arrived with 2F98, the 22:40 service from Ebbw Vale Parkway, on 2 October 2013. The unit would then run empty to Canton depot for servicing prior to starting services all over again the next day.

The route to Bridgend from Cardiff via Barry and the Vale of Glamorgan skirts the coast every now and again, particularly near Aberthaw and the caravan parks at Fontygary. In this shot, No. 150281 heads along the coast at Aberthaw while working 2E36, the 13:38 Merthyr Tydfil to Bridgend service, on 20 January 2017.

First published 2018

Amberley Publishing
The Hill, Stroud
Gloucestershire, GL5 4EP

www.amberley-books.com

Copyright © Nicholas Wilcock, 2018

The right of Nicholas Wilcock to be identified as the Author of this work has been asserted in accordance with the Copyrights, Designs and Patents Act 1988.

ISBN 978 1 4456 8199 3 (print)
ISBN 978 1 4456 8200 6 (ebook)

British Library Cataloguing in Publication Data.
A catalogue record for this book is available from the British Library.

Origination by Amberley Publishing.
Printed in the UK.

Introduction

October 2018 brings with it the end of Arriva Trains Wales holding the contract for the Wales & Borders franchise. Although Arriva had bid to renew their contract, they pulled out of the running in late 2017, leaving three companies in the running: Abellio, Keolis Amey and MTR Corporation. The collapse of the Carillion engineering group in early 2018 led to Abellio pulling out of the franchise race. In May 2018, the contract was awarded to the Keolis/Amey joint venture, which will run the Wales & Borders franchise for a fifteen-year period under the Transport for Wales brand. New trains are in the pipeline along with new stations, station improvements and an increase in services with the Valley Lines network seeing the most significant changes as part of the planned South Wales Metro.

The aim of this book is to provide a pictorial record of Arriva Trains Wales operations over the course of the franchise. Being a South Wales, and predominantly Cardiff, based photographer, many of the photographs included within are from around South Wales. With this in mind I will take you on a journey through South Wales, starting along the banks of the River Severn. Upon reaching Newport we take a trip up the Marches line to Shrewsbury before heading back south again to the main line, taking in Ebbw Vale en route. Once at Cardiff we head up the Valley Lines network, first covering the branches north of the main line followed by those to the south. The South Wales Main Line is then covered west of Cardiff Central with a diversion via the Maesteg branch on the way. Our trip ends in the Llanelli area after a little jaunt up the Heart of Wales line.

I have tried to keep the captions informative, although I have kept the history side brief as many books have already been written covering the history of Welsh railways.

History

Owned by the German railway company Deutsche Bahn, Arriva Trains Wales (or Trenau Arriva Cymru as it is called in Welsh) is one of the many subsidiaries of Arriva Trains UK and has been operating nearly all the railway services across Wales since 2003, when it was awarded the franchise that had been previously run by Wales & Borders – a franchise that had been formed from Wales & West, Valley Lines and the Central Trains-operated Cambrian services. The First North Western services, which ran in North Wales, were transferred over to Arriva not long after they started. The services that aren't operated by Arriva Trains Wales include South Wales to London and the South West, which are run by Great Western, North Wales to London, run by Virgin, and Cardiff to Nottingham and Manchester (via Birmingham), run by CrossCountry.

During the period of the franchise, passenger numbers have grown significantly to approximately 30.5 million per year and this has seen lines reopened to passengers and a couple of new stations added to existing routes. In 2005, the Vale of Glamorgan line west of Barry reopened to passengers with stations being built at Rhoose (for Cardiff Airport) and Llantwit Major. Llanharan was then opened in 2007 followed by the reopening to passengers of the Ebbw Vale branch with intermediary stations being built at Pye Corner, Rogerstone, Risca & Pontymister, Crosskeys, Newbridge and Llanhilleth. Not all of the stations opened with the line's reopening and initially the terminus was at Ebbw Vale Parkway, just south of the town; however, in 2015 the line was extended through to a new terminus nearer the centre. West Wales welcomed a new station in 2012 at Fishguard & Goodwick. The Valleys network also saw the opening of a new station in 2013 at Energlyn & Churchill Park on the Rhymney line, as well as significant changes to Abercynon South station in 2008, which became simply Abercynon following the closure of the nearby North station and associated track remodelling.

Arriva operate 1,015 services per day covering just over 1,000 route miles through a total of 247 stations (10 per cent of the UK total), covering the whole of Wales and extending to Crewe, Manchester Piccadilly, Bidston on the Wirral Peninsula, Birmingham International, Gloucester and Cheltenham. In the early days, London Waterloo, Brighton, Portsmouth Harbour and Penzance were served by ATW, although these are now served by First Great Western, with Waterloo being covered by South West Trains, now South Western Railway. In 2010, Arriva applied to run an Aberystwyth to London Marylebone service but the application was rejected.

The Fleet

The Arriva Trains Wales fleet is made up of 125 diesel multiple units (DMUs) along with three Class 67 locomotives, which are hired in from DB Cargo, twelve Mark 3 coaches and three Mark 3 driving van trailers. The fleet has varied over the years as units have moved around different operators. The thirty Class 142 and 143 Pacers have remained a constant throughout, along with the eight Class 153 'bubble cars'. The Class 150 fleet has increased, with units having been received from ScotRail, One, First Great Western and Central Trains, and they currently stand at thirty-six units. Class 158s total twenty-four, with some of those having been swapped between operators, while the full, twenty-seventy-strong Class 175 fleet came to Arriva via First North Western although a number were leased back until they received their own new units in 2006. Once the full complement of Class 175s was back in Arriva's hands, a number of Class 158s headed off for pastures new.

For a short time, a heritage Class 121 'bubble car' was part of the fleet for use on the Cardiff Bay branch, although following a major failure and the increased unreliability prior to that, the unit was withdrawn from service. That wasn't the end for it though as it now resides on the Wensleydale Railway in North Yorkshire.

Y Gerallt Gymro/Gerald of Wales or Premier Service

In December 2008, and having bid for it alongside the Wrexham, Shropshire & Marylebone Railway and Grand Central, Arriva Trains Wales introduced a new weekdays loco-hauled service connecting North Wales with South Wales between Holyhead and Cardiff.

Run under contract to the Welsh Assembly Government (WAG), it initially ran under the name 'Y Gerallt Gymro/Gerald Of Wales', although it is more commonly referred to as the WAG – or certainly within railway enthusiast circles at least. It was later rebranded as the Premier Service, although nowadays it is marketed as the Business Class Service as a way to entice those travelling to Cardiff for work from the north.

At the time of writing, the train leaves Holyhead at 5.30 a.m. and, having travelled down the Marches route, arrives in Cardiff shortly before 10 a.m. Following servicing at Cardiff Canton during the day, it returns north again at 17.15, arriving back in Holyhead at 21.40. Originally, the WAG left Cardiff an hour earlier in the evenings and ran via Crewe, but the introduction of DVTs on the train saw it rerouted via Wrexham with a reversal at Chester.

When not in use on the weekends the stock stables at Holyhead, and so it is often called upon to provide extra capacity when there are large sporting events on in Cardiff's Millennium Stadium.

The WAG is Arriva Trains Wales' only service to offer first-class seating. Passengers who pay the premium for travelling in first class get to enjoy the benefits of a full, freshly cooked breakfast on the southbound journey and a three-course meal on the evening northbound journey, all cooked using locally sourced ingredients.

When the Premier service was first introduced, the train was formed of three standard class Mark 2 coaches that had been refurbished at Eastleigh Works and a Mark 3 first/buffet coach and was hauled by one of four Class 57/3 locomotives that had been hired in from Virgin (Nos 57313–316); however, it was not uncommon in the early days for the train to be double-headed or top and tailed as it was a convenient way of getting the locos back to their home depot for servicing. All four Class 57s gained Arriva's base blue/turquoise livery, with Nos 57314 and 57315 gaining full Arriva Trains Wales branding.

From March 2012, Arriva replaced the Class 57s with three Class 67 locomotives (Nos 567001–003), which were hired in from sister company DB Schenker. These locos also gained Arriva's base livery. They were initially used with the original Mark 2/Mark 3 stock; however, from September 2012, the Mark 2s were replaced by Mark 3 coaches that had been overhauled by Pullman Rail in Cardiff, along with one of three Mark 3 driving van trailers (DVT), which allowed the train to run in push/pull formation.

It is in this formation that the WAG currently runs, although reliability issues have seen the dedicated locos returned to DB Schenker (DB Cargo as it's now known), with traction now coming from any of DB's available Class 67s. Arriva's own Class 175 DMUs will sometimes substitute if the loco-hauled set is unavailable for any reason. The loss of the Arriva-liveried Class 67s has brought about a welcome variety of liveries on the front (or rear) of the train, with some of those being pictured in the coming pages.

Other Loco-Hauled Services

The Premier Service is not the only loco-hauled service to have been operated by Arriva Trains Wales over the course of the franchise. Currently a weekday diagram is operated along the North Wales Coast between Manchester and Holyhead utilising a Class 67 hired from DB Cargo with another Mark 3 set with a DVT. The only difference between this set and the WAG is the lack of catering facilities. A similar service also operated for a short time in 2006, using hired in Virgin Class 57/3s and Mark 2s due to the poor availability of Class 175s.

Far and away the most well known and most fondly remembered loco-hauled services were those that ran on the Rhymney Valley line that had been inherited from Valley Lines. Two services, Monday to Friday, would run down into Cardiff from Rhymney first thing in the morning, returning again in the evening peak. The stock would stable at Cardiff Canton during the day, so during the summer holiday season one of the sets would get used for an out and back trip to Fishguard Harbour to connect with the ferry to Ireland. The Fishguard trains first ran in 2002, prior to ATW taking over, using Class 37s and ran until the summer of 2006, by which point they were in the hands of Class 50s, although units were used for the summer 2005 season. For three days in July, however, the Fishguard service reverted back to a unit as the stock was used to increase capacity on the Heart of Wales line for the duration of the Royal Welsh Show at Builth Wells. These trains would run direct from Rhymney to Llandrindod Wells via Cardiff and the Swansea District line – a distance of approximately 120 miles by rail as opposed to approximately 50 miles direct by road.

In addition to the weekday workings, ATW would use the loco-hauled sets all day on a Saturday between Cardiff and Rhymney to free up a couple of units for use elsewhere. In the latter days, you have to wonder how many passengers on the weekend workings were shoppers and how many were enthusiasts spending the day building up their mileage tally!

At one time Arriva had a fleet of approximately twenty Mark 2s and this allowed them to operate top and tailed shuttle services between Newport, Cardiff and Swansea when there were sporting events on at the Millennium Stadium. These were hauled by Class 37s from EWS, Class 47s from Freightliner or Riviera Trains and Class 50s from The Fifty Fund (No. 50031) or Project Defiance (No. 50049). Loco-hauled services in the Rhymney Valley were scheduled to cease with the commencement of the winter timetable in December 2005, and to celebrate this Arriva marked the occasion with a farewell event on the first Sunday of the month. All services to Rhymney were top and tailed by locos that had been associated with the line over the years; namely, Classes 33, 37, 47 and 50.

West Coast Railways supplied Nos 33207 and 47854, No. 50031 *Hood* was supplied by The Fifty Fund with No. 50049 *Defiance* being supplied by Project Defiance, while the English, Welsh & Scottish Railway provided No. 37411 *Caerphilly Castle/Castell Caerffili*, No. 37419 and No. 37425 *Balchder y Cymoedd/Pride of the Valleys*. A special day rover ticket was available and, as was expected, services were well patronised.

In the end, it proved not to be the last loco-hauled service in the Valleys as they returned for a short time a couple of months later; this time, however, it really was for the last time.

The ending of the Rhymney services wasn't to be the end of loco haulage in South Wales as, for a couple of weeks in December 2005, top and tailed 37s were used on Cardiff to Gloucester workings for a week followed by a week of trips to Fishguard Harbour as a result of a DMU shortage. Football/rugby specials would continue for a further couple of years.

Carrying the old Visit Wales advertising livery, No. 150282 heads south on 13 April 2005 along the banks of the River Severn at Purton with a Gloucester to Cardiff service.

The once sprawling yards and loco stabling point at Severn Tunnel Junction are now just a distant memory. There is still some evidence left of their existence in this shot of No. 150252 as it slows for its stop while on a Cheltenham-bound service on 28 April 2014; namely, the old shed building which can be seen just above the unit.

Above and below: Having worked one of the morning services from Rhymney to Cardiff on 9 December 2005, No. 37405 was paired up with No. 37411 *Caerphilly Castle/Castell Caerffili* to work two round trips between Cardiff and Gloucester prior to resuming their Rhymney duties to free up a DMU for use elsewhere as Arriva was suffering from availability issues with its units at the time. The pair ran top and tailed using one of the sets of stock from the Rhymney services and are first recorded heading south at Purton with 2G67, the 14.45 Gloucester to Cardiff Central service, and heading north earlier in the day at Lydney with 2G64, the 13.10 Cardiff Central to Gloucester.

Prior to their introduction on the WAG, one or two of the dedicated Class 67s would travel down to Cardiff from their home in Crewe for driver training. This would be undertaken at Cardiff's Canton Depot and often involved an out and back run to Gloucester. No. 67003 heads east through Severn Tunnel Junction on 29 March 2012 on one of these runs.

Although Arriva Trains Wales doesn't operate any services in the Bristol area any longer, sister company Arriva Train Care has a facility at Barton Hill, just north of Bristol Temple Meads, which Arriva Trains Wales has the use of. Moves to and from Barton Hill are generally the only occasions when ATW units could be seen on the English side of the Severn Tunnel over recent years. On 12 July 2014, No. 142081 takes the line towards the tunnel at Severn Tunnel Junction on one such move from Cardiff Canton to Bristol Barton Hill.

On 20 August 2012, a lone passenger crosses the old footbridge at Severn Tunnel Junction having alighted from No. 158839, which was working a Cheltenham to Cardiff Central service. The bridge was replaced in 2016 by a much larger and more imposing structure complete with ramps to comply with the latest regulations.

2017 saw the introduction of Great Western's new bi-mode Class 800 IETs and that brought about an increase in civil engineering work along the length of the South Wales Main Line between Cardiff and the Severn Tunnel in preparation for the impending electrification work. The vast majority of the road bridges crossing the main line have had to be replaced by higher structures to accommodate the extra clearance needed for the overhead wires. The work to the bridge providing access to the Severn Bridge tolls, etc. can be seen on 24 June 2017 as No. 150280 pauses at Severn Tunnel Junction while working 2G54, the 08.00 Maesteg to Cheltenham Spa. The old road bridge, which crossed the original yard, stood for many years and was always popular with enthusiasts as it was a great vantage point. Unfortunately, the new bridge, which opened in October 2017, has significantly higher parapets, requiring the use of steps to be able to see over; whether it remains a popular spot is yet to be seen!

On 14 March 2016, No. 150251 is seen heading east at Llandevenny while working 2G54, the 07.59 Maesteg to Cheltenham Spa. In the background is the well-known Bishton Flyover, where the Up relief line crosses over the Up and Down main lines. East of the flyover, at Severn Tunnel Junction, the Up and Down yards were on the north and south side of the main lines. When Llanwern steelworks began operation, the four-track section towards Cardiff was altered so that the relief lines were on the south side of the main lines to allow the flow of iron ore from Newport Docks to be kept clear of the main line all the way to Llanwern. The flyover was constructed in 1961 to take the Up relief back to the north side of the Up main to avoid conflicting movements across the main lines for traffic accessing the Up yard.

No. 143623 is seen passing the site of the former Undy halt while working 2L59, the 13.45 Cheltenham Spa to Maesteg service, on 14 March 2016. Opened in 1933, the halt was made up of two short wooden platforms with a small waiting shelter on each and served the main lines, with the relief lines passing on either side. The halt was closed in 1964.

Half a mile to the west of Undy was Magor station. It originally opened much earlier than Undy, in the very early days of the South Wales Main Line in 1850. Like Undy, it too closed in 1964. In this shot taken on 22 May 2017, No. 158822 passes the site of the former station while working 2G56, the 09.16 Maesteg to Cheltenham Spa. With the growth of Magor and Undy over recent years, there have been campaigns to open a new station to serve the growing population, which stood at approximately 500 when both stations were closed and is predicted to grow to nearly 10,000 over the coming decade. In 2016, a funding application for £5.2 million was submitted by Monmouthshire County Council and the Magor Action Group on Rail to the Department for Transport to go towards the cost of the proposed £7 million new station, with the balance hopefully being provided by the Welsh Government. To date, nothing has come of the application, and proposals for new stations in South Wales didn't include Magor.

Still carrying the colours of its former operator, First Group, No. 175111 takes the curve onto the Marches line at Maindee West Junction having just departed Newport with an unknown northbound working on 30 May 2006.

Although more commonly in the hands of Class 150 or Class 158 units, the services to Gloucester and Cheltenham can see any of Arriva's fleet of units put into action. On 7 December 2014 it was the turn of No. 142082, which is seen passing Maindee West Junction, Newport, with a Cardiff-bound service.

With the St Julians area of Newport forming the backdrop, 1V91, the 05.33 Holyhead to Cardiff, rounds Maindee West curve as it comes off the Marches line propelled by No. 67002 on a gloomy 9 December 2014. Along with Maindee east curve and the South Wales Main Line, Maindee west curve forms what is known locally as the Maindee triangle and this area is often used for turning the loco-hauled sets (primarily the buffets) or sometimes just the DVTs as needed. It is also regularly used to turn steam locos that come into South Wales on charters bound for Cardiff. The east curve now only sees freight traffic, although in the late 1990s/early 2000s a few passenger services would use the curve, thus avoiding a reversal at Newport.

No. 57316 pulls into Abergavenny with the 1W91, Cardiff Central to Holyhead WAG, on 19 March 2012.

The driver of No. 57316 awaits the 'right away' at Abergavenny while working the final northbound Class 57-hauled 1W91, the Cardiff Central to Holyhead WAG service on 23 March 2012.

Above and below: The North and West or Marches route is one of the last remaining outposts for semaphore signalling in South Wales. Abergavenny has plenty, especially on the southern approach to the station, as visible in these shots of DVT No. 82307 leading No. 67001 on 1W96, the 17.16 Cardiff Central to Holyhead on 11 September 2015.

Arriva Trains Wales' Class 175 units provide the main traction for services on the Marches and they are represented here by No. 175104, seen at Hereford while working 1W91, the 07.21 Cardiff Central to Holyhead service, on 7 April 2016. As well as being served by Arriva's North Wales and Holyhead services, Hereford also sees regular services to Birmingham via Worcester, provided by London Midland (now West Midlands Trains), as well as services through to London Paddington via Worcester and Oxford, provided by First Great Western.

Shrewsbury station is a significant junction on the Arriva Trains Wales network and still boasts an impressive signal box and array of semaphore signals. Here, services from Aberystwyth and Pwllheli combine with services from Holyhead to continue on to Birmingham International while services from South Wales either fork off to Chester and Holyhead or Crewe and Manchester. The station is also served by West Midlands Trains and Virgin. Heart of Wales services also terminate at Shrewsbury and four hours after setting off on 26 January 2017, No. 153327 is pictured in the bay platform having worked 2M08, the 09.33 from Swansea to Shrewsbury.

The December 2005 timetable change saw quite significant changes and to promote this, a few of Arriva's units were rebranded with 'Times Are Changing'. The sole Class 158 to carry this livery was No. 158841 and it is seen crossing the River Usk at Newport with a westbound service on 30 May 2006.

In crisp winter sunshine, No. 142081 crosses the River Usk having just departed Newport on a Cheltenham-bound service on 7 December 2014.

DB's silver-liveried No. 67029 *Royal Diamond* has been a regular substitute for the Arriva 67s over the years and it is seen here at Newport with 1W96, the 17.16 Cardiff Central to Holyhead, on the evening of 16 February 2015. No. 67029 gained its name and silver paint job back in late 2004, when the English, Welsh & Scottish Railway introduced its Managers Train for corporate usage and as a mobile office. When EWS were bought out by DB Cargo, the original 'three beasties' logo on the side was removed and replaced with DB's own branding, as seen here.

Over recent years Arriva Trains Wales has partnered up with Pathfinder Railtours to take rugby fans from South Wales to Edinburgh on the occasions that Wales play Scotland at Murrayfield in the Six Nations tournament. Departing on the Friday morning, the charter allows fans the full weekend in Edinburgh to take in the match and sights before returning back to South Wales by Monday night. Traction was originally provided by EWS using their Class 67s; however, more recently Direct Rail Services has been the traction provider, using a variety of their locos. For the 2015 trip, one of DRS's new Class 68 locomotives was used for the first time. It's this trip that is recorded here on 16 February 2015 at Newport as No. 68005 *Defiant* sets down passengers from 1Z69, the 07.10 return from Edinburgh to Carmarthen. This particular charter also saw the first Class 68 to work west of Cardiff after two of the Chiltern-liveried locos worked down a few months prior. And for those who may be interested, Wales beat Scotland 26-23.

Nos 153303 and 153353 get the green as they prepare to leave Newport while working 2G66, the 16.15 Maesteg to Cheltenham Spa, on 26 January 2017.

Carrying the livery of sister company DB Schenker, No. 67015 pauses at Newport on the evening of 26 January 2017 with 1W96, the 17.16 Cardiff Central to Holyhead.

In 2010, Newport station saw a significant redevelopment, which was completed to coincide with the Ryder Cup golf tournament being held at the nearby Celtic Manor resort. The most imposing change was the installation of a new footbridge at the Cardiff end of the station. A slightly earlier makeover for the station saw Platform 4 brought back into use at Newport. On 27 February 2014, No. 175114 pauses while working a Manchester Piccadilly-bound service.

A busy scene at Newport on 20 March 2005 as former North Western-liveried Nos 153313 and 150284 pause while on an unidentified working.

Still carrying the base silver livery from its previous owners, Wales & West, No. 158830 pauses at Newport on 20 March 2005 while working a Cardiff Central-bound service.

Passengers alight from No. 175003, which is working to Milford Haven on 27 February 2014, at Newport.

Riviera Trains No. 47815 (formerly named *Abertawe/Landore*) brings up the rear of 1Z47, the 12.25 Cardiff Central to Holyhead ruggex, as it enters Hillfield Tunnel just to the west of Newport station on 20 March 2005. Fellow celebrity No. 47847 was hauling the train, although this later failed at Rhyl so No. 47815 was tasked with providing power for the remainder of the journey. The match the previous day brought about a close to the 2005 Six Nations Championship and saw Wales beat Ireland at home by 32 points to 20 to become the winners of the Championship and the Grand Slam.

The 770-yard-long Hillfield tunnels at Newport were constructed to take the South Wales Main Line beneath Stow Hill. The first tunnel was built by Brunel and was opened in 1850, with the second one being built sixty years later. Former Central Trains-liveried No. 158853 exits the 1910-built northern tunnel on 4 March 2006 on a westbound working.

Following many years as a freight-only branch, and following the closure of the steelworks in 2002, the line to Ebbw Vale was reopened to passengers in 2008. The line originally terminated at Ebbw Vale Parkway and No. 150252 is pictured here waiting to leave with 2F38, the 13.39 to Cardiff Central, on 21 January 2015. The station is 2 miles away from the town centre and so later that year the line was extended up to a new terminus at Ebbw Vale Town. The reopening of the line saw new stations being opened, including Rogerstone, Risca & Pontymister, Crosskeys, Newbridge and Llanhilleth, with Pye Corner being added in 2014.

A very popular spot for photography along the South Wales Main Line is the Hawse Lane road bridge in Coedkernew. Pioneer No. 67001 is depicted here on 11 September 2015 while en route to Cardiff with 1V91, the 05.33 from Holyhead.

In the late afternoon sunshine, No. 175114 is pictured at Coedkernew on an unidentified westbound service on 20 August 2012.

The final Class 57-hauled WAG service passed by without any fanfare, although an extra coach had been added to cater for folk wanting to travel behind it. It is seen here passing Coedkernew on the morning of 26 March 2012. No. 67002 had the honours of hauling the return working that evening, thus becoming the first Class 67 to haul the Premier Service.

Recently repainted No. 158825 heads west along the Down relief at Coedkernew on 28 March 2012.

Prior to their introduction in September 2012, drivers undertook training on the Mark 3 DVTs so another round of driver training trips commenced between Cardiff and Gloucester. One of these trips is seen here at Coedkernew on 19 July 2012, returning from Gloucester, running as 5Z63 to Cardiff Canton with No. 67002 pushing No. 82306 along the South Wales Main Line.

With France playing Wales at the Millennium Stadium on 27 February 2005, shuttle services were laid on between Newport and Cardiff to help ease traffic around Cardiff. In the final shot from Coedkernew, No. 143604 and its partner in former Valley Lines livery head towards Cardiff on one of their many trips between the two cities.

On the final approaches to Cardiff Central, former First North Western-liveried No. 175108 is viewed from the footbridge at Pellett Street while heading west on 25 February 2006.

Although not one of my better shots, I have included this photograph taken on 27 February 2012 of No. 57315 working 1W91, the 16.15 Cardiff Central to Holyhead, passing under the line to Cardiff Queen Street from the bridge at Pellett Street as it is the only shot I have of a 57 carrying the full Arriva livery. No. 57314 was the only other one out of the four hired to carry the full livery. Both Nos 57313 and 57316 carried a plain variation, as depicted earlier.

One of my favourite locations to watch trains go by is the roof terrace of Jacob's Antiques Centre in Cardiff. A fantastic view can be had of traffic passing through Cardiff Central while enjoying a cup of tea and a piece of cake from the café downstairs. In this busy scene from 11 October 2014, Arriva's No. 150213 heads toward Cardiff Queen Street on a Bargoed-bound service while No. 66200 passes on the main line with the Aberthaw Power Station to East Usk coal empties. In the background, Nos 20303 and No. 20304 await a path through Cardiff Central while working Pathfinder's 1Z28 Derby to Llandrindod Wells 'Heart of Wales Explorer' charter.

On 18 April 2015, Nos 150245 and 150285 set off from Cardiff Central on a service to Merthyr Tydfil while No. 150216 makes its way down from Queen Street to terminate. On this particular occasion Valleys services were terminating at Cardiff Central as the Penarth Curve was closed for engineering work.

The various Pacers that work around the country have some slight variances between them, some of which are more noticeable than others. One of the differences that's only noticeable from above is the ribbing on the roof, as visible on No. 142075 and an unknown classmate seen leaving Cardiff Central on a Treherbert-bound service on 22 September 2012. No. 142075 is now a unique member of the class as it subsequently lost its roof pods.

Above and below: A good comparison of two variants of the Arriva livery which are shown to good effect here on 9 September 2012 as No. 158821 carrying the current livery departs Cardiff Central while No. 158818 represents the older livery as it arrives at with a westbound working.

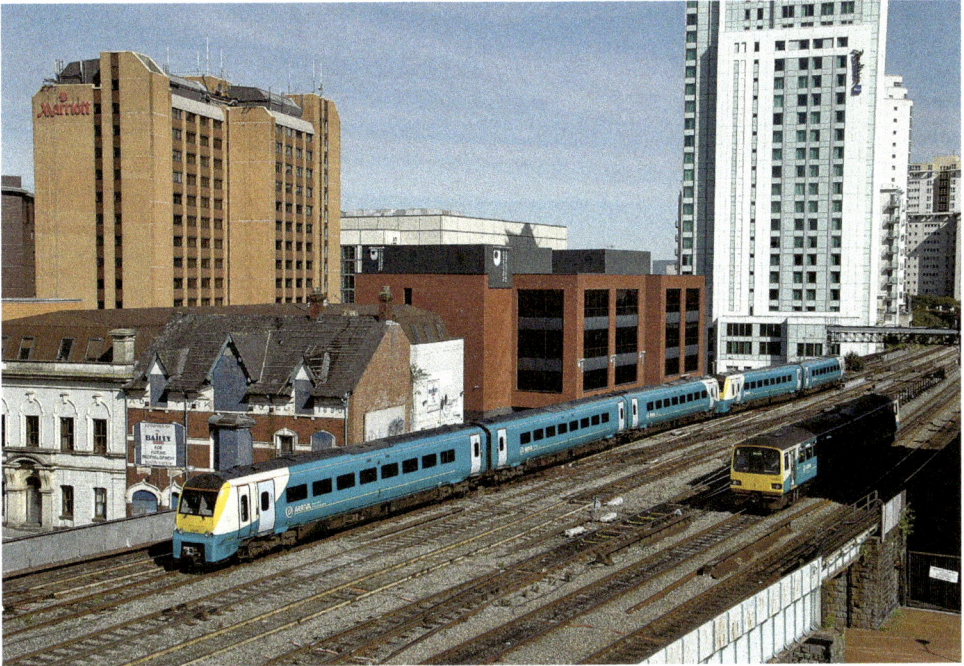

On 22 September 2012, No. 175115 and an unidentified Class 175/0 depart Cardiff Central as No. 142622 heads to Queen Street on a City Line service. This scene has changed as the old York Hotel has now been demolished, and in the not too distant future the overhead lines will significantly change the view.

No. 150236 approaches Cardiff Central with a service bound for Bridgend via the Vale of Glamorgan line on 30 May 2012.

For many years Cardiff Central was made up of six platforms, with two of those being dedicated for use by the Valley Lines services. In 1999, that number rose to seven with the construction of Platform 0 on the north side of the station. On 30 May 2012, No. 150252 awaits departure with a service bound for Ebbw Vale.

Full house at Cardiff Central on 30 May 2012 as No. 175116 arrives with an eastbound service while No. 175010 awaits departure to the west. No. 150252 stands in Platform 0 with an Ebbw Vale service.

In the period when Arriva used its Class 67s with the original Mark 2 and Mark 3 coaching stock, No. 67002 is seen snaking over the pointwork at the west end of Cardiff Central as it brings the empty coaching stock over from Cardiff Canton on 30 May 2012 prior to working up to Holyhead.

Autumn 2015 saw the Rugby World Cup being held in the UK, with matches held at various venues around the country, including Cardiff's Millennium Stadium. On 19 September 2015, Ireland played Canada in Cardiff, so many services were strengthened, leading to busy scenes at the platforms. Showing the original and current liveries, Arriva Nos 150213 and 150241 share platform space with an unidentified First Great Western Class 158 and Class 150 combination awaiting departure to the east.

As the late evening sun breaks through a stormy sky, No. 153353 awaits a path back to the depot at Canton having spent a day on City Line services on 20 June 2014.

To mark Arriva Trains Wales' tenth anniversary, No. 150213 was adorned with commemorative vinyls to mark the occasion. It is seen at Cardiff Central on the evening of 20 June 2014 with a service bound for Rhymney with No. 142077.

As the light begins to drop, No. 142081 pauses at Cardiff Central while working 2C43, the 17.04 Radyr to Coryton, on 2 March 2017.

On the morning of 3 April 2017, unbranded DB Schenker-liveried No. 67010 departs Cardiff Central with 5V91, the 10.06 empty coaching stock off the Holyhead service to Cardiff Canton Depot.

A well-known feature at the west end of Cardiff Central is the Grade II listed Great Western water tower, which was built in 1932. For many years it carried a mural of daffodils, but in 2012, after they faded and the tower looked weather-beaten, Network Rail repainted it into Great Western colours. On 7 July 2017, No. 143608 passes the tower as it arrives in Platform 0 in readiness to work 2N09, the 09.34 Cardiff Central to Ebbw Vale Town.

After working the 2B38 1245 Llanelli to Cardiff Central, No. 153303 awaits departure back to Cardiff Canton on 17 July 2017. Originally built as two-car Class 155 units in the late 1980s by Leyland Bus, the Class 153s came into being to replace the ageing Class 121 and 122 fleet, after the decision was made to convert the Class 155s into single-car units. Hunslet Barclay in Kilmarnock was awarded the contract and the new, modern-day bubble cars went into service in 1991/2.

No. 142081 seems to be one of the Pacers that I've captured on camera a few times over the years. On 14 October 2017, it's seen at Cardiff while working 2H13, the 12.32 Penarth to Ystrad Mynach.

Working 1V39, the 10.30 Manchester Piccadilly to Milford Haven, No. 175001 attracts the attention of a couple of enthusiasts on 16 October 2017. The station was full of enthusiasts on this particular occasion as the first of Great Western's Class 800 IETs was due in on its first run in public to Swansea.

Arriva's hybrid Class 150 Sprinter No. 150978 stands in Platform 0 at Cardiff Central prior to working 2N23, the 16.34 service to Ebbw Vale Town, on 14 December 2017. This unit was formed after No. 150217 collided with a fallen tree at Llanbradach in September 2017. With Arriva being short of units, the undamaged half of No. 150217, DMS No. 57217, was inserted into No. 150278 to form a three-car set – a first for Arriva. It was generally confined to main line workings off Cardiff and could be found on Swansea services, Maesteg to Cheltenham services, Cardiff to Ebbw Vale services and occasionally Marches services. Following repairs at Wolverton, DMSL No. 52217 of No. 150217 returned to Cardiff Canton in January and both sets were reformed, with No. 150978 being disbanded.

2017 ended with the WAG in the hands of EWS-liveried No. 67016 and it is seen here awaiting departure from Cardiff Central on the evening of 14 December 2017.

On a warm Saturday 17 September 2016, shoppers alight from No. 153367 as it pauses at Cardiff Central while working a City Line service to Radyr. Visible on the right of the shot, the new Platform 8 is nearing completion.

Having worked down from Holyhead, and still carrying its original EWS livery, No. 67022 is seen departing Platform 4 at Cardiff Central with the empty coaching stock bound for Arriva's depot at Canton on 22 September 2016.

Left: The backdrop to Cardiff Central has changed drastically over recent years, with numerous office blocks and high rise buildings springing up on the adjoining site of the former bus station. Number One Central Square towers above Nos 153312 and 153303 on 25 October 2016, which, along with No. 150262, were awaiting departure with 2N23, the 16.34 Cardiff Central to Ebbw Vale Town.

Below: In January 2017, Platform 8 was opened at Cardiff Central to ease congestion as part of a modernisation scheme. Penarth, Barry and Bridgend via Rhoose services use the new platform and on a rainy 20 March 2017 No. 150231 approaches with 2P47, the 12.00 Bargoed to Penarth service.

Above: As mentioned previously, the now defunct Wrexham, Shropshire & Marylebone Railway was one of the bidders for the Premier Service. They also used Class 67s on their services to London and it is one of their former liveried locos, No. 67012, which is pictured here awaiting departure from Cardiff Central on 2 March 2017.

Right: There's no mistaking the location of this photograph! No. 158838 is seen at Cardiff Central while working 2G60, the 12.17 Maesteg to Gloucester, on 4 September 2017.

On St David's Day 2012, No. 67002 is held at Cardiff Central having been out on a Cardiff Canton to Cardiff Canton via Gloucester driver training run.

No. 150257 stands at Cardiff Central on 18 February 2014 with the last train of the day to Penarth – 2P99, the 21.54 service from Aberdare.

Above and below: DVT No. 82306 leads 1V91, the 05.33 from Holyhead, into Cardiff Central on a dull 31 October 2017, with No. 67015 providing the traction at the rear. No. 67015 was one of DB's Class 67s that gained house colours without branding, though it eventually gained branding with some extra advertising as seen here.

My dad and I were lucky enough to be granted access to the roof of the Altolusso tower block in Cardiff to get some slightly different shots of Arriva's loco-hauled specials on 4 December 2005. At the time of the following photographs, the block was the tallest residential building in Wales, standing at a height of 232 feet, and it offered a fantastic view of the trains leaving Cardiff Canton, passing through Central and then on up to Queen Street. In this first shot, No. 37425 *Balchder y Cymoedd/Pride of the Valleys*, with No. 37419 bringing up the rear, departs Cardiff Central with 1Z36, the 11.56 to Rhymney.

The above shot sees BR green-liveried No. 37411 *Caerphilly Castle/Castell Caerffili* with Project Defiance's No. 50049 *Defiance* heading away from Cardiff Queen Street with 1Z33, the 12.15 Rhymney to Cardiff.

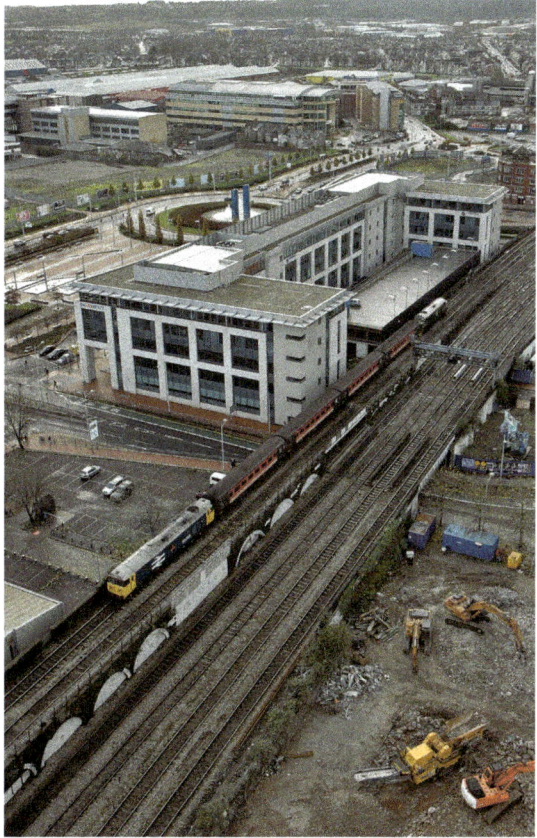

With the Grangetown area of Cardiff in the background, Nos 37411 and 50049 pass the offices of ING Direct and Eversheds on the final approach to Cardiff Central, from where they'd run down to Cardiff's Canton depot to reverse.

The University of South Wales' Cardiff campus dominates the background as No. 37425 *Balchder y Cymoedd/Pride of the Valleys* rounds the curve from Cardiff Central on the approach to Cardiff Queen Street while working 2R34, the 14.59 Cardiff Central to Rhymney, on 3 December 2005. The track on the far left of the picture is that of the short branch to Cardiff Bay.

The driver of No. 37419 awaits the 'right away' at Cardiff Queen Street while working 2R30, the 13.59 Cardiff Central to Rhymney, on 3 December 2005.

On a busy October half term afternoon, passengers attempt to board an already busy No. 142002 at Queen Street, which was working 2A38, the 14.41 Barry Island to Aberdare service. In December 2014, two new platforms were opened, or in the case of Platform 5 pictured here, reopened, at Cardiff Queen Street to increase capacity. The other new platform was constructed to give the Cardiff Bay services their own dedicated platform, allowing them to shuttle back and forth without any impact on the rest of the station.

The aforementioned platform for Cardiff Bay services can be seen to the right of this photograph of No. 142081 at Queen Street working 2P40, the 11.00 Bargoed to Penarth service, on 3 April 2017. The original station that was built here was named Crockherbtown and was constructed by the Taff Vale Railway in 1840. It gained its current name after being rebuilt in 1887. It underwent further work in 1907 and then 1973, with the latter rebuilding seeing the most significant changes, including the removal of the overall roof.

Formerly named Cardiff Bute Road, Cardiff Bay is served by a 1-mile branch from Queen Street station and for a short time it gained popularity with enthusiasts as Arriva employed one of the last remaining first generation DMUs for the three-minute journey. Unfortunately, I never managed to photograph it at work, so the branch service is represented here by No. 153320 on 3 April 2017 as it waits to leave with 2S52, the 11.54 service to Cardiff Queen Street.

Left: On 12 April 2005, No. 37425 was outshopped by EWS's Toton Depot in the classic BR large logo livery, and three days later it found itself back in traffic on the Rhymney services. It is pictured here departing Cardiff Queen Street on 15 April with its first passenger working in large logo blue – 2R38, the 16.50 Cardiff Central to Rhymney. Later in the year, it was named *Balchder y Cymoedd/ Pride of the Valleys* at Caerphilly in a joint ceremony with No. 37411, which received the name *Caerphilly Castle/Castell Caerffili*.

Below: The short branch to Coryton diverges off the Rhymney line a few miles north of Cardiff Queen Street at Heath Junction. Having worked 2C31, the 14.04 service from Radyr, No. 153362 is seen at journey's end on 25 October 2016 prior to returning back as 2V33, the 14.45 service to Radyr. The Coryton branch is known as the City Line and carries a half-hourly service along the single-track branch that originally carried on to Tongwynlais prior to its closure in 1952.

Following an incident at Rhymney, which is pictured later, Arriva hired in locos and rolling stock from Riviera Trains. No. 47839 was the first of the Riviera locos to work up to Rhymney and it is seen here arriving at Caerphilly with 2R38, the 16.50 Cardiff Central to Rhymney, on 9 August 2005.

With No. 33207 for company, West Coast Railway's No. 47854, complete with recently fitted snowploughs, pauses at Caerphilly while working 1Z28, the 09.56 Cardiff Central to Rhymney service, on 4 December 2005.

The December 2005 gala day not only proved to be a big day for Arriva, but also a big day for No. 33207, which is recorded at Caerphilly on the rear of the working in the preceding photograph. The day's activities were the Class 33's first workings for WCRC following its purchase from Direct Rail Services, as well as its first passenger workings for quite some time.

BR green-liveried No. 37411 *Caerphilly Castle/Castell Caerffili* is pictured shortly after departing Pontlottyn with 2F26, the 12.15 Rhymney to Cardiff, on 10 December 2005.

Right: The first 'final' loco-hauled service, the 20.20 Rhymney to Cardiff Central, was on 10 December and was worked by No. 37419. Celebrity large logo blue-liveried No. 37425 had been earmarked to work the last train, but on the day it was out of traffic undergoing a 'B' exam. Earlier in the day, No. 37419 is seen from Hill Road, Pontlottyn, while crossing the viaduct with 2R26, the 12.59 Cardiff to Rhymney.

Below: After working up from Cardiff on the evening of 1 August 2005, No. 37408 *Loch Rannoch* ran away from the headshunt at Rhymney while performing shunt duties and collided with a set of stock in the yard, damaging both the loco and the stock. Unfortunately, this bump proved to be the end for No. 37408, as it was put into storage for some time at Toton before being officially withdrawn and cut up at EMR Kingsbury in January 2008. No. 37425 also suffered minor damage, but was back in service a month later.

On the evening of 16 May 2013, No. 142083 departs Taffs Well with a Cardiff-bound service. Taffs Well used to be a busier location for railways as it was a junction for the nearby Nantgarw Colliery, the original Rhymney Railway via Aber Junction and the main line to Pontypridd. A factory complex and engine shed also stood alongside the station and both remain to this day; though for how much longer remains to be seen, as it has been proposed to redevelop the site as a depot for the new South Wales Metro system, which should come to fruition in the coming years.

In a burst of sunshine on an otherwise grey day, No. 150231 slows for its stop at Mountain Ash while working 2Y41, the 11.22 Aberdare to Barry Island service, on 24 February 2017. The Aberdare line branch from Abercynon is largely single track, although a loop was installed here when the 1988-built station was rebuilt in 2002.

No. 150213 stands at the 'new' Aberdare station on 27 January 2015 prior to working 2Y41, the 11.22 to Barry Island. Passenger services through to the original High Level station ceased in 1964 under the Beeching cuts, although the line remained open for coal traffic from Hirwaun and Abercwmboi. Passenger services resumed in 1988 and the current station was built just short of the previous one.

The original Aberdare High Level station is visible in the background of this shot of No. 150254 awaiting departure with 2Y49, the 12.52 Aberdare to Barry Island service, on a dull 23 February 2017. No. 66547 can also be seen awaiting a clear path to head south with 6C45, the Tower to Aberthaw Power Station working. Coal workings from Tower would cease the following day. The original High Level station is currently undergoing restoration to become part of the new Coleg y Cymoedd campus.

Above and below: The penultimate stop on the Aberdare branch is Cwmbach. The current station was opened in 1988 and extended in 2005, although there was a halt on the site that was opened by the GWR in 1914 and closed in 1964. Taken the day before the previous photograph, No. 143609 *Sir Tom Jones* and No. 142010 are depicted heading south at Cwmbach with 2Y49, the 12.52 Aberdare to Barry Island, crossing the Afon Cynon just south of the station.

Above and below: In the final picture from the lines north of Cardiff we see No. 150278 at Treherbert on 23 February 2017 prior to departure with 2F54, the 14.47 service to Cardiff Central. The sidings where units are stabled overnight can be seen in the first picture. The second photograph shows the station looking north-west, with the headshunt to access the stabling point in the background. The headshunt is all that remains of the line towards the collieries at Blaenrhondda, which closed in the late 1970s.

Heading south now out of Cardiff, the first station is Grangetown, which is where the Ferry Road freight branch split off until it was lifted in the late 1980s. The last remnants of the embankment from Grangetown were flattened during 2017 to make way for housing. Now devoid of its tenth anniversary vinyls, No. 150213 sets off on 15 March 2016 with a service bound for Barry Island.

Nos 142077 and 143608 are pictured crossing the River Ely from Grangemoor Park, in between Grangetown and Cogan, on 1 March 2017.

As mentioned on one of the earlier photographs, No. 142075 became a unique member of the Pacer fleet after it lost its roof pods, giving it quite a different look. The difference is quite apparent in this shot as it approaches Dingle Road station on the Penarth branch with No. 142083, forming 2P49, the 12.17 Bargoed to Penarth, on 20 March 2017.

Nos 142075 and 142083 are seen again approaching Dingle Road when returning from Penarth with 2D40, the 13.18 service to Bargoed.

Above and below: No. 150231 is pictured at Dingle Road on 20 March 2017 while working 2P47, the 12.00 Bargoed to Penarth, and then again returning with 2R12, the 13.02 Penarth to Rhymney. The station was opened by the Taff Vale Railway in 1904 and originally had two platforms. The Down platform was closed in 1967 and is still just about visible under the vegetation today.

Having arrived with 2P57, the 13.28 service from Ystrad Mynach, the driver of No. 143622 (with No. 143624) changes end at Penarth prior to working back out as 2D46, the 14.18 service to Bargoed, on 17 September 2016. In its heyday Penarth had two platforms as well as a small yard, and the branch continued through Lavernock and Sully before joining the line to Barry at Biglis Junction to the east of Cadoxton. However, passenger services west of Penarth were withdrawn in 1968, with the remaining freight traffic ceasing the following year.

On the evening of 27 February 2014, No. 143609 *Sir Tom Jones* stands at Penarth with 2T56, the 19.47 service to Treherbert.

No. 150241 is seen at Cogan on 6 March 2017 while working 2A40, the 14.42 Bridgend to Aberdare. The branch from Penarth comes in from the right just beyond the two bridges.

No. 150280 pauses at Eastbrook on the Cardiff to Barry line with an Aberdare-bound service on 1 March 2014.

The line between Cardiff and Bridgend via Barry is often used as a diversionary route whenever the main line is closed for engineering work. On one such occasion, No. 175112 is seen passing through Dinas Powys with the diverted 1V16, the 14.30 Manchester Piccadilly to Milford Haven service, on 21 May 2017.

On 18 November 2014, No. 150279 picks up passengers at Cadoxton while working to Bridgend via Rhoose. The railway to the east of Cadoxton at one time split, providing two routes to Cardiff (via Dinas Powys or via Penarth) and also a route through Wenvoe up to Porth and Pontypridd. To the west of the station, a freight-only branch drops away from the main line to serve the once extensive Barry Docks complex.

Nos 142085 and 142077 approach Barry Docks station while working 2Y43, the 12.56 Cardiff Central to Barry Island service, on 17 June 2014.

In 2014, as part of a scheme to improve capacity, a third platform opened at Barry to serve trains heading towards Barry Island while trains to Bridgend continued to use Platform 2. The new platform line is bi-directional and is sometimes used to allow late-running trains to omit Barry Island and make up some time by heading straight back to Cardiff, as shown here as No. 150229 prepares to leave Barry with a Merthyr-bound service on 20 September 2014.

Above and below: The following two images show services approaching Barry as seen from the Barry Tourist Railway's yard. The first shot shows Pacers Nos 142082 and 143609 *Sir Tom Jones* working 2Y43, the 12.56 Cardiff Central to Barry Island service, on 9 July 2014 while the second one depicts No. 150235 working 2Y31, the 09.51 Aberdare to Barry, on 30 September 2014.

Working a Barry Island service, the driver of No. 150253 changes the destination blind at Barry in readiness for its return working on 22 August 2015.

No. 150259 approaches Barry from the Vale of Glamorgan line with 2A36, the 13.42 Bridgend to Aberdare service, on 17 June 2014. The points on the left lead to the Down goods loops.

Above: Barry's new Platform 3 can be seen nearing completion on 17 June 2014 while No. 150259 departs while working 2A36, the 13.42 Bridgend to Aberdare service. A major resignalling scheme in South Wales saw the closure of the 117-year-old signal box here only ten days after this photograph was taken, though it wasn't demolished until early 2015.

Right: No. 150241 slows for its Barry stop while working 2E28, the 11.38 Merthyr Tydfil to Bridgend service, on 1 July 2014.

No. 143608 stands at Barry on 11 October 2016 with 2Y61, the 14.51 service from Aberdare to Barry Island. This was another service that had terminated short of its destination and returned back towards Cardiff as 2M46, the 16.30 service to Merthyr Tydfil. In the rear of the photograph, Colas' No. 37116 can be seen in the Barry Tourist Railway's yard, where it had arrived to collect a couple of stored barrier vans.

In crisp, winter sun on 18 January 2015, No. 150255 is seen departing Barry while working 2E40, the 09.38 Merthyr Tydfil to Bridgend service.

With the destination blind already changed in readiness for its return journey to Aberdare, No. 150251 departs Barry station on 5 August 2012 and takes the branch to Barry Island.

Strictly speaking, Barry Island is no longer an island as it was linked to the mainland in 1896 by a 250-yard-long causeway. No. 150264 is seen crossing the causeway on 6 May 2012 as it nears its destination having worked down on a service from Aberdare. The branch to Barry Island is now single track, but the causeway is still double track as one of the lines is used by the Barry Tourist Railway, who run services from Barry Island to either Hood Road or Gladstone Bridge halts.

On a busy August bank holiday, No. 142075 stands at Barry Island prior to working 2M38, the 14.26 Barry Island to Merthyr Tydfil, on 31 August 2013.

As No. 142075 waits to leave Barry Island, 1908-built GWR steam railmotor No. 93, which is based at the Didcot Railway Centre, sets off on a round trip on the Barry Tourist Railway. Some might say that the railmotor is a very distant relative to the 1980s-built Pacers as they were used on similar services when new.

Barry Island station was opened in 1896 and was always busy, with day trippers and holiday makers from the Valleys and further afield visiting the nearby Pleasure Park, Butlins and beaches, and although its heyday is long gone, trains in the summer months can still be well loaded, especially on a sunny day! The original station building, which is visible in this wider angle, still stands and though it is not used by passengers off Valleys services, it is now used as the headquarters for Cambrian Transport who run the Barry Tourist Railway, having taken over the lease from the Vale of Glamorgan Railway in 2009.

Briefly hit upon earlier was the fact that Arriva used a heritage Class 121 bubble car, No. 121032, on the Cardiff Bay branch. The unit was introduced in mid-2006 and prior to introduction a number of driver training trips were run over the Arriva network and the Vale of Glamorgan Heritage Railway at Barry Island. The only photographs I managed to get of No. 121032 were on one of the occasions it was at Barry, and it is pictured on 19 July 2006 at the Plymouth Road station on the Vale of Glamorgan Railway during a break in the day's training. Entry into service was a month later. The bubble car lasted until 2013, when it was eventually withdrawn after it became more and more unreliable and parts became scarce. Thankfully she found a new home in preservation at the Wensleydale Railway in North Yorkshire and she has also been immortalised in model form.

Shortly after leaving Barry, the Vale of Glamorgan line crosses over the impressive 376-yard-long, 1897-built Porthkerry Viaduct. During a weekend of diversions on 14 May 2017, an unidentified Class 150/2 heads east with 1W26, the 15.15 Milford Haven to Manchester Piccadilly service. On clear days passengers on the south side of the train get a superb view of the Bristol Channel and the northern coast of Somerset.

The Vale line also meets the coast as it passes the caravan park at Fontygary shortly after passing Cardiff Airport. The former Aberthaw lime works, which is now a nature reserve, is visible just off the beach while the large chimney is part of the Aberthaw Power Station complex. In winter sunshine on 29 December 2014, No. 150254 heads west with 2E24, the 10.38 Merthyr Tydfil to Bridgend service.

The same spot at Fontygary as viewed from the beach shows the caravan park off to good effect. On 20 January 2017, No. 150281 heads along the coast while working 2E36, the 13.38 Merthyr Tydfil to Bridgend service.

No. 150236 passes the reception sidings at Aberthaw while working 2A40, the 14.42 Bridgend to Aberdare, on 8 April 2016. Following the South Wales resignalling programme, the signal box in the background became redundant, but unlike the box at Barry it has remained in situ on the platform of the old Aberthaw station, which closed along with many others in 1964. The reception sidings for the power station were once a busy place, with coal coming from numerous sources around South Wales to feed its hunger, but in March 2017 that chapter was brought to a close when the last trainload of Welsh coal arrived behind No. 66511. Up until very recently, coal continued to be delivered, but was sourced from Russia arriving via Avonmouth; however, these trains have now stopped for the time being.

Having climbed the bank from Aberthaw, No. 150285 passes near RAF St Athan with 2E56, the 18.38 Merthyr Tydfil to Bridgend service, on 27 June 2014. This wide view shows off Aberthaw Power Station on the right on the coast and Aberthaw Cement Works on the left. Just about visible on the horizon to the left of the cement works are the white buildings of Cardiff International Airport and the large British Airways maintenance facility, which see regular visits by the larger planes in their fleet.

Another view of the older Valley Lines livery and one of the named units as No. 143605 *Crimestoppers* heads west at St Athan on 12 July 2005 with a Bridgend-bound service. Arriva has had a few named units throughout its franchise period, although most of those were carried over from the previous franchise. Only one unit now retains a name – the previously pictured No. 143609 *Sir Tom Jones*.

In June 1964, the Vale of Glamorgan line between Barry and Bridgend was closed to passengers as part of the Beeching cuts; however, the line remained open as a diversionary route and for freight traffic serving Aberthaw Power Station and the Ford engine plant at Bridgend, which was accessed via the Vale branch. Forty years later, work began to bring the line back into passenger use, and that included the construction of new stations at Llantwit Major and Rhoose (to serve Cardiff International Airport), as well as reinstating the bay platform at the east end of Bridgend station for the termination of Vale services. The line was officially reopened on 10 June 2005, with services starting two days later. On the first day of services, No. 142082 (with No. 142074) pauses at Llantwit Major with a Bridgend-bound service.

The Vale line passes through largely rural areas, especially west of Llantwit Major. On 1 August 2017, No. 143625 heads east at the little hamlet of Castle-upon-Alun while working 2A36, the 13.42 Bridgend to Aberdare service.

Above and below: To mark the reopening of the Vale of Glamorgan line and connection with the Barry Transport Festival, Arriva Trains Wales laid on a number of loco-hauled extras using a spare set of Rhymney stock top and tailed by celebrities Nos 37411 and 37425. After working Rhymney, the pair made a couple of round trips along the Vale and took in the Cardiff Bay line. The pair are pictured at Llantwit Major while working the last extra of the day – 1Z44, the 17.20 Bridgend to Rhymney.

Back on the South Wales main line, Valley Lines-liveried No. 143624 and an unidentified Class 143 carrying an old Bristol advertising livery head back to Cardiff Central on 10 April 2005 having reversed at what is known the Brick Yard or old parcels depot opposite Canton Depot. The building they are spotted alongside was latterly used as a freight depot but was demolished in 2010 to make way for the new South Wales signalling centre at Canton.

Still carrying First North Western livery, No. 175109 is pictured on the approach to Cardiff Central at Canton with an eastbound service on 25 February 2006.

No. 150264 was one of a number of Class 150/2s that were transferred to Cardiff from Scotland in early 2005, and on 11 March 2005 it shows off the livery of its previous owners to good effect as it heads down the Brick Yard at Canton to reverse. Services that arrive in Cardiff from the east use the Brick Yard to reverse to clear platform space at Central.

Valley Lines-liveried No. 143604 passes under the footbridge at Cardiff Canton on 23 April 2004 while working a Maesteg to Coryton service.

Taking a break from Royal Train duties, No. 67006 *Royal Sovereign* passes Cardiff Canton depot while working 1Z50, the 08.05 Swansea to Edinburgh ruggex, for Arriva in conjunction with Pathfinder Tours on 11 March 2005. Fans were taking the over eight-hour journey north to see Wales play Scotland at Edinburgh's Murrayfield Stadium. Wales went on to beat Scotland 46-22, setting them on their way to winning the Six Nations Championship.

Prior to Arriva taking on the South Wales franchise, five of the Class 158s were given Ginsters advertising and they retained their branding for a good few years into the new franchise. One of the units is pictured on 13 December 2005 at St Georges, west of Cardiff, on an unknown westbound service.

One of the former Central Trains-liveried Class 158s heads west at St Georges on 13 December 2005.

As previously mentioned, the Fishguard Harbour services reverted to loco haulage for a week at the end of 2005. In low winter sun on 13 December 2005, No. 37411 *Caerphilly Castle/Castell Caerffili* heads west at St Georges with 1B96, the 10.55 Cardiff to Fishguard Harbour.

In one of the earlier variations of the Arriva livery, No. 158818 passes through this picturesque spot at St Georges while heading towards Cardiff on 11 March 2006.

It's 11 March 2006 and it's another rugby day in South Wales, which means more loco-hauled shuttle services. Project Defiance's No. 50049 and the Class Fifty Fund's No. 50031 head east at St Georges with a Bridgend to Newport shuttle. In 2006, the two groups agreed a merger and the following year the Class 50 alliance was formed. The group, based at the Severn Valley Railway in Kidderminster, now look after five locos, with Nos 50007 and 50049 currently being passed for main line use. For those with an interest in such things, Wales were playing Italy at home, with the game ending with a score of 18-18.

One my favourite spots for photography on the South Wales Main Line has always been the level crossing at Pontsarn, as there was always a good view of services passing by. On 24 February 2016, Nos 142002 and 153327 head east at Pontsarn with 2B38, the 13.10 Swansea to Cardiff Central service, which was originally booked to start at Llanelli.

As with many other locations, the vegetation has now taken over at Pontsarn, and in the summer months the options are very much limited to a near enough head-on view of services heading east, as depicted by No. 175104 on 6 June 2015.

Working 2L52, the 10.16 Maesteg to Cardiff Central service, No. 158840 is seen heading east through Miskin on 28 January 2016. This is another location that has changed drastically over the years as it wasn't that long ago that it was possible to see the M4 motorway in the background. Now, even in the winter months when there are no leaves on the trees, you wouldn't know the motorway was there if it wasn't for the constant road noise.

No. 175109 heads east at Pontyclun with an unknown working on 19 April 2015. The land to the right of the unit was the site of the former Llantrisant Yard until the mid-1980s, and a connection off the main line, which used to carry traffic from Cwm Colliery, remained in place until around 2006/7. It had been used at the very end of its life by Freightliner for stone traffic, but it was very short lived.

Pontyclun station was opened in 1992 on the site of the former Llantrisant station, which closed in 1964, and is mainly served by services to and from Maesteg. On 24 February 2017, No. 158827 sets off from Pontyclun with 2L49, the 08.46 Cheltenham Spa to Maesteg service.

Looking east at Pontyclun, No. 143605 departs with a Maesteg to Cheltenham service on 26 May 2016.

On 15 August 2017, No. 150267 calls at Pontyclun while working 2L54, the 13.15 Maesteg to Cardiff Central service.

With XP64-liveried No. 47853 *Rail Express* providing the power up front, No. 47843 *Vulcan* brings up the rear of 1Z12, the 12.19 Port Talbot to Cardiff ruggex, as it heads east through Pontyclun on a dismal 5 November 2005. Fans were making the trip to Cardiff to see Wales get beaten by New Zealand, 3-41. No doubt the mood on the return trip was somewhat different to the mood earlier in the day! The former crossover to access the yard and branch to Cwm Colliery can be seen just to the right of the loco.

In 2007, and following much campaigning from residents of the village, Llanharan station was opened on the site of the former station, which had fallen victim to the Beeching cuts of 1964. The station is typical of those built to meet access standards, with large ramps snaking their way down from the car park. They are just visible on the right of No. 158819, which is pictured slowing for its stop on an eastbound service on 19 July 2013.

Looking east at Llanharan on 27 June 2014, No. 150283 pauses with a Maesteg-bound service.

Above and right: On 30 May 2014, No. 150257 slows for its stop at Pencoed while working 2L51, the 11.20 Cardiff Central to Maesteg service. Along with many other stations on the South Wales Main Line, the original station was closed in the cuts of 1964. The present station was opened in 1992 in conjunction with the reinstatement of services to Maesteg.

Taken on the same day as the previous shots, No. 158830 is seen at Pencoed while working 2G58, the 11.15 Maesteg to Cheltenham service.

On the evening of 26 January 2017, No. 175114, working 2L56, the 18.20 Maesteg to Cardiff Central, is seen at Bridgend passing No. 150278 on 2L65, the 16.46 Cheltenham Spa to Maesteg. The Brunel-designed station was opened in 1850 and, along with the footbridge, is Grade II listed.

Having come off the Maesteg branch at Llynfi Junction, No. 150257 slows for its stop at Bridgend with a Maesteg to Gloucester service on 30 May 2014.

Tondu station on the Maesteg branch north of Bridgend was once a significant railway junction, with branches converging from Bridgend, Port Talbot, the Ogmore Valley and the Garw Valley. Traffic in the area was so great that a large engine shed was sited to the north of the station. Although it survived the Beeching era, Tondu closed to passengers in 1970 and the platforms fell into a state of disrepair until it was reopened in 1992. No. 150260 is captured by my dad, Michael Wilcock, a well-known videographer and YouTuber in South Wales, as it departs towards Bridgend with 2L54, the 13.15 Maesteg to Cardiff Central service, on 24 June 2016.

Left: Tondu has always been popular with photographers, especially when a charter visits, as it retains numerous semaphore signals protecting Tondu Middle Junction. No. 150256 edges towards the signal box to gain the token for the remainder of the Maesteg branch while working 2L55, the 13.19 Cardiff Central to Maesteg, on 24 June 2016.

Below: A good comparison of variants of Class 150 units is visible in this image of Arriva No. 150256 working 2G62, the 14.15 Maesteg to Cheltenham Spa service, as it passes Network Rail's track recording unit No. 950001, which is stood in the rarely used Llynfi loop at Tondu while working 2Q08, the Cardiff Canton to Cardiff Canton via Abercynon, Bridgend Ford, Tondu and Margam, on 24 June 2016. The track that disappears off to the right is the last remnant of the branch that went up to Pontycymer, which closed in 1997, while the track that is just about visible coming in from the left is that of the branch to Port Talbot. They are still just about in use as freight can be diverted this way via a reversal when the South Wales Main Line is closed between Bridgend and Margam.

Above and below: The line through the Lynfi Valley originally carried on north through Maesteg to Abergwynfi but after the demise of coal traffic in the late 1980s it became the terminus when the line reopened. Although only a small town, Maesteg is lucky enough to boast two stations with Maesteg Ewenny Road being situated just over a mile away. On 19 August 2014, No. 150236 is seen at journey's end after working 2L57, the 14.21 service from Cardiff Central. From here it returned with 2G64, the 15.19 service to Cheltenham Spa.

The next series of photographs are taken from a bridge on a minor road at Llangewydd, just to the west of Bridgend on the eastern approach to Stormy Bank. On 21 April 2014, No. 158829 heads west while working 1B96, the 10.40 Newport to Fishguard Harbour service.

Llangewydd is a scene that changes vastly through the year with the coming and going of the seasons. In the summer months, the old farm building on the left practically disappears under the vegetation, only to reappear when everything dies back in the winter. On 15 May 2014, No. 175115 heads east with an unidentified working.

Taken on the same day as the previous photograph, No. 175003 heads east towards Bridgend on an unknown working. The backdrop to this view has significantly changed now as a rather large solar farm has been built in the fields to the left.

Having frequented this location, it's been fascinating to see the gradual decline of the barns at the farm on the right and the increase in the lineside vegetation. The difference is noticeable in this photograph, which is dated two years prior to the previous one, depicting No. 142010 heading west with a Swansea service on 11 May 2012.

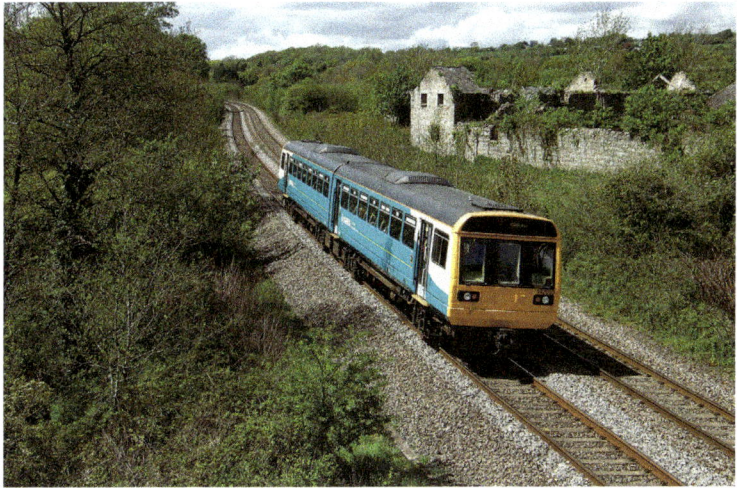

No. 175010 nears the top of Stormy Bank on the South Wales Main Line a few miles west of Bridgend while working 1W64, the 13.02 Carmarthen to Manchester Piccadilly, on 10 March 2017. The loops at the summit of the bank are just out of shot under the bridge in the background.

Early 2017 saw the clearance of the lineside vegetation alongside Stormy Bank and that has opened up the shot for trains climbing the bank bound for the east. On 10 March, No. 153353 heads east with 2B38, the 1245 Llanelli to Cardiff Central. The bridge the previous photograph was taken from can be seen in the background.

On 31 May 2014, No. 175103 hurries through Baglan station on an unidentified eastbound service. In 1994 an hourly Cardiff to Swansea service was launched under the Swanline branding and served new stations opened nearer Swansea at Pyle, Briton Ferry, Skewen and Llansamlet, with Baglan being added to the service in 1996. Low passenger numbers have seen the service, now no longer officially called Swanline, reduced to a two hourly service, with a few extra services calling in the morning.

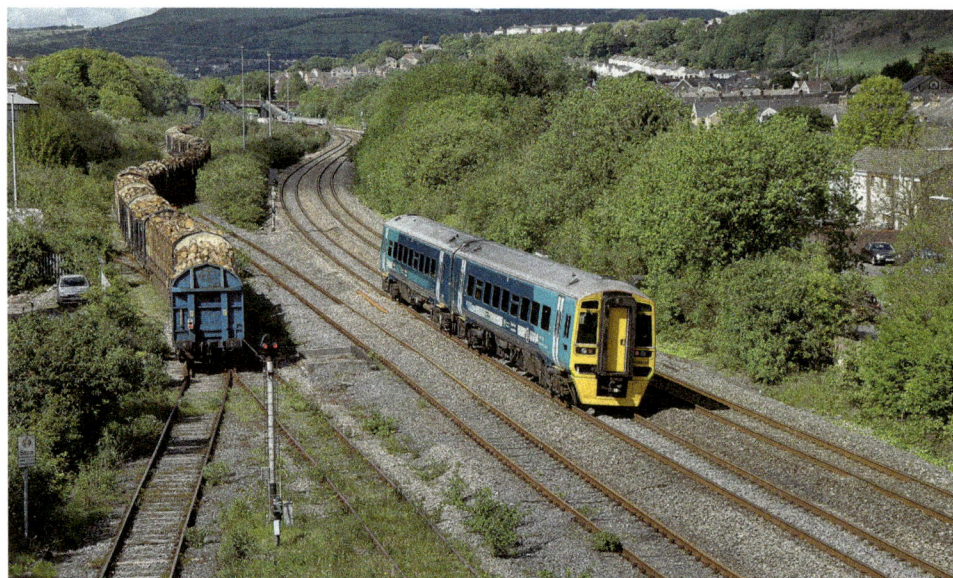

No. 158834 heads west at Briton Ferry while on a westbound service on 13 May 2014. The once busy yard to the left of the station is now largely overgrown, and after being unused for some time is now used by Colas Railfreight, who use the yard to run round the Baglan Bay to Chirk timber trains and to stable the wagons for the stone traffic from Neath Abbey Wharf. One of the former can be seen making its way into the yard from Baglan Bay, which on this occasion was hauled by Nos 56078 and 56113.

All services to and from West Wales, with the exception of a couple of Fishguard Harbour trains, must reverse at Swansea, and one such service – 1V31, the 04.50 Crewe to Milford Haven – is pictured here on 26 January 2017 in the hands of No. 175104.

Journey's end for No. 153362 *Dylan Thomas 1914–1953* as it stands at Swansea on 27 February 2014 having arrived with 2V39, the 14.05 service from Shrewsbury via the Heart of Wales. It would then form 2M65, the 18.21 service back north.

No. 175004 heads west having just crossed the Loughor Viaduct (just out of shot on the right) on 24 March 2012. This section of line between Cockett West and Duffryn Junction was redoubled the following year to allow for an increase in capacity after it had been singled in the mid-1980s, and it also saw the renewal of the viaduct, strengthening the structure.

Arriva's Pacers aren't a particularly common sight west of Swansea, but they do appear from time to time. On one such occasion, No. 143610 is seen heading towards Swansea alongside the A484 at Loughor on 24 March 2012.

Trains to and from the Heart of Wales have to reverse at Llanelli to be able to serve Swansea. Although it is possible to access the Heart of Wales branch without this reversal, it is only from the Swansea District line at Hendy Junction, and so it misses Swansea. Passenger services use this connection for a couple of days in July when Arriva put on a relief service from Cardiff to take passengers to the Royal Welsh Show. Having worked down the Heart of Wales line, No. 153362 *Dylan Thomas 1914–1953* reverses at Llanelli while working 2V39, the 14.05 Shrewsbury to Swansea, on 27 February 2014.

Showing its advertising livery off to good effect, 'Visit Wales' branded No. 150279 arrives at Llandovery on 25 June 2005 with a Shrewsbury/Crewe-bound working. In the background, D1015 *Western Champion* and No. 37427 draw forward into the station while working 1Z56, the Llandrindod Wells to Exeter leg of Pathfinder's mammoth Western Trident charter, which had originated at London Euston the previous day and ended at London Victoria the next day.

No. 153362 *Dylan Thomas 1914–1953* stands at Llandovery on 27 February 2014 while working 2V39, the 14.05 Shrewsbury to Swansea. The early months of the year are a good time to take a trip on the Heart of Wales as passengers are rewarded with better views as a result of the lack of foliage on the trees, and I had subsequently taken the chance to have a trip using a Heart of Wales circular ticket.

On a very cold 26 January 2017, No. 153367, working 2V08, the 09.14 Crewe to Swansea, is seen passing No. 153327 (which I was travelling on) at Llandrindod Wells, which was working north on 2M08, the 09.33 Swansea to Shrewsbury.

Although Arriva Trains Wales operates from the upper depot at Cardiff Canton, on 4 December 2005 the lower part of Cardiff Canton, operated by Pullman Rail, was used to turn the Rhymney loco-hauled specials around and for service if required. Here, No. 37425 *Balchder y Cymoedd/Pride of the Valleys* prepares to head back to Cardiff Central to work 1Z48, the 14.56 service to Rhymney, with No. 37419 bringing up the rear. No. 50049 *Defiance* takes a break from the day's activities having given its place up to No. 50031 *Hood*.

Towards the end of the loco-hauled 'gala' day in the Rhymney Valley on 4 December 2005, No. 37419 takes a break at Cardiff's Canton depot after working 1Z49, the 16.15 Rhymney to Cardiff Central, with No. 37425. My dad and I were lucky enough to be invited down to the depot by the late Tom Clift, a gentleman who played a key role in putting loco-hauled trains on the Rhymney services.

11.30 p.m. and all's quiet as No. 150252 stands at a deserted Cardiff Central having arrived with 2F98, the 22.40 Ebbw Vale Parkway to Cardiff Central Arriva Trains Wales service, on 2 October 2013.

Arriva Trains Wales' fleet is based at Cardiff Canton along with depots at Chester and Machynlleth and they are supplemented by numerous stabling points around their network. During its layover, No. 67029 *Royal Diamond* is pictured on 17 July 2017 from a passing Penarth train while the WAG stock is serviced.

About the Author

My interest in railways started in the early 1980s when my dad used to take me to Cardiff station to keep me entertained while my mum went shopping. The seed was planted and my love of railways was cemented. I started off, as many young boys do, by taking down numbers until I was given an SLR camera for my thirteenth birthday, and over the years I became more interested in the photography side of the hobby.

Back then I didn't take so many detailed notes to go with my photographs, but with the improvement in technology and the information that's available, I now like to get as much information as possible to accompany my photographs.

I took a break from the railway scene to pursue other interests, but I returned to the hobby with renewed interest to fill my time while temporarily out of work. Thankfully I now have a view of the railway from my place of work, so I can get a daily fix of railway action.

If you would like to view more of my photographs, head over to my page on Flickr: www.flickr.com/photos/nickwilcock.

Acknowledgements

I would like to take this opportunity to thank a few people who have helped me along the way.

Firstly, thanks to my parents, Mike and Avriel, my brother Andrew and my partner Jill, who have all offered their encouragement with this project and who have had to endure many hours sat by a railway line at some obscure location over the years, as well as having shopping trips and days out interrupted by trains.

Secondly, I would like to thank the various folks out there on the railway forums and Facebook pages who provide the 'gen' day in, day out. The information that is held within such circles is greatly appreciated.

Finally, I'd like to thank the staff at Amberley Publishing for giving me the chance to put my photographs into print.

References

Books
Kenny, Adrian, *Railways of South Wales* (Ian Allen Publishing, 2010).
Morgan, Jeff and Eldridge, Wayne, *Welsh Railways – A New Perspective* (Bernard McCall, 2010).

Websites
Arriva Trains Wales (www.arrivatrainswales.co.uk)
Railway Correspondence & Travel Society (www.rcts.org)
Wikipedia